To ....

From ....

Other books by Gregory E. Lang:

WHY A DAUGHTER NEEDS A DAD

WHY A SON NEEDS A MOM

WHY A SON NEEDS A DAD

WHY I LOVE GRANDMA

WHY I LOVE GRANDPA

WHY I CHOSE YOU

WHY I LOVE YOU

WHY MY HEART STILL SKIPS A BEAT

WHY A BABY NEEDS A MOMMY

WHY WE ARE A FAMILY

WHY WE ARE FRIENDS

GOOD LUCK, GRADUATE

BROTHERS AND SISTERS

SIMPLE ACTS

LOVE SIGNS

LIFE MAPS

THANK YOU, MOM

THANK YOU, DAD

BECAUSE YOU ARE MY DAUGHTER

BECAUSE YOU ARE MY SON

WHY A *Son* NEEDS A *Dad*

100 REASONS

Gregory E. Lang

with photographs by Janet Lankford-Moran

CUMBERLAND HOUSE

Published by Cumberland House, an imprint of Sourcebooks, Inc.
P.O. Box 4410, Naperville, Illinois 60567–4410
(630) 961–3900 Fax: (630) 961–2168
www.sourcebooks.com

Printed and bound in China
OGP 10 9 8 7 6 5 4 3 2 1

On behalf of my brothers, David, Kevin, and Jody, and myself, this book is lovingly dedicated to Jacobs Eugene Lang, our dad.
——Greg

To John, my husband/photo assistant, thank you for your encouragement and patience.
——Janet

INTRODUCTION

I am the first-born child of a household that included five children before my dad was thirty years old. Ours was the house that never seemed to sleep, with constant activity swirling around it and within it, the one that seemed nearly to burst at the edges as the children who called it home continued to grow. My dad worked hard to provide for his family, but also made time to be with his children, both together and one-on-one. He made sure the tree house we built ourselves was sturdy and safe, that my soapbox racer would indeed cross the finish line, and that once big enough to see over the steering wheel, each child, sitting in his lap, got a chance to drive through the neighborhood in their choice of the station wagon or the old pickup truck.

I have many heartwarming memories from my youth: my dad showing me how to hit a curveball in the front yard; working with Dad on a Boy Scout project to earn a coveted merit badge; handing him his tools as he tinkered with the car or improved the house on a Sunday afternoon. My dad loved to fish. I remember being awakened by him before sunrise on Saturday mornings, and whispering so as not to awaken my younger siblings, the two of us slipping outside to go fishing. Standing at the water's edge we sometimes talked. Other times we were both content just to listen to the morning sounds. In these early years of my life, my dad was my hero.

As I became a teenager our relationship began to change. Like most young people, I considered myself misunderstood and overly controlled. I wanted to wear the "in" clothes and stay out late with my friends, shirking my chores and other responsibilities. My demonstrations of rebellion irritated my dad like a pesky splinter under a fingernail. Both being strong willed, my dad and I clashed often. My stormy coming-of-age years were difficult for both of us. At times our disputes were serious enough that I questioned our love for one another, and I wondered what happened to the man who had taught me how to fish. When I left home I promised myself I would not be like him when I became a man, and most certainly not when I became a father.

By the time I entered graduate school my dad and I had come to a peaceful coexistence. We were different, but we could get along. We would not talk much, but we would not argue either. The emotion between us was warm, but not embracing. I could thank him for the money he would slip into my pocket when he thought I wasn't looking and for welcoming me as I came home now and then for one of Mom's soothing Sunday meals. He could tell me he was proud of what I had accomplished. Our relationship was not what it had been, but it was such that I could love him again. This will be okay, I thought to myself. I did not imagine then that years later we would find ourselves sharing a deep bond, that I would feel intensely for him, and that I would be giving my dad credit for helping to shape me into the man I would become.

Today, with more years and a few hundred thousand miles under my feet, I have come to see my father very differently. Now being a father of an emerging teenager and experiencing for myself the stresses and challenges I must have presented in my youth, I smile when I realize my daughter and I are playing out the same debates and negotiations my father and I once did. Now, wiser, I know it was not that I was misunderstood or controlled, but that I lacked the life experience to know what risks I was taking, the judgment to get myself out of trouble before a permanent scar might be made, and the understanding that it was possible something bad could happen to me. Today I know my dad was protecting me from what I could not see and simply trying to save himself from the gut-wrenching fear of allowing his child to let go of his hand.

A dad has the responsibility of providing for his family. Sometimes the difficulties of that task go unrecognized and without gratitude. Now having that responsibility for myself—and for only one child, I might add—I look back in amazement at what my dad did. He sometimes worked two jobs to support his family; he pushed himself beyond his education to acquire the skills necessary for a better career; and he never bought things for himself before he took care of his children. We ate well, dressed warmly, received gifts, and went on vacations. Even today he continues to extend help to his adult children when he thinks it is needed. I have called him in the middle of the night and he has come to me.

On my mantel, next to a high school portrait of my mom and amid many photographs of my daughter, sits a picture of my dad and me in the front yard of my parents' first house. He is squatting down, his arms wrapped around me as I stand between his knees. Sometimes as I reflect on what is important to me, I stand before this mantel and look at those photographs, realizing how blessed I am to have these loving parents and this wonderful child. As I think of the difficult years of my youth, I think that perhaps I owe my parents, especially my dad, an apology, but know that they would wave me off and accuse me of being silly. I think of things I would like to do for them, and I look forward to each time I hurry my daughter into the car and make a trip to the home I left so many years ago. I am eager to get there, to kiss Mom, and to sit on the front porch and talk with Dad.

Now having come full circle as a son who once worshipped, then disfavored, and now deeply admires his dad, and being a father trying my best to parent but finding myself always second-guessing my abilities, I wonder if my teenage daughter will ever look at me with dancing eyes again. I think the role of being a dad is the greatest challenge and the highest reward a man can have. Reflecting on my dad and me, I know my child and I will have a wonderful, loving, and long-lasting relationship because my dad and I have one. I know that in the end I will be satisfied with my performance as a father because my dad showed me how to do it. And I can believe that I have been a good son because my dad tells me so. I love you, Dad, I do. And I am proud to be your son.

WHY A

Son

NEEDS A Dad

100 REASONS

A

Son

· *Needs a* ·

DAD

···

TO SHOW HIM HOW TO SHAVE.

···

to teach him how to talk to girls.

A

Son

· Needs a ·

DAD

TO TEACH HIM TO BE A GRACIOUS WINNER
AS WELL AS A GRACIOUS LOSER.

·

to show him how to be

productive with his hands.

A

Son

· *Needs a* ·

DAD

*to listen when others
have grown tired of listening.*

TO TELL HIM THAT ALL IS NOT HOPELESS,

EVEN WHEN IT MAY SEEM THAT IT IS.

A

Son

· *Needs a* ·

DAD

WHO WILL EXPECT HIM TO PLAY FAIR.

•

to teach him to treat women with kindness.

•

TO TEACH HIM THAT MEN
AND WOMEN ARE EQUALS.

A

Son

· Needs a ·

DAD

to prepare him for being
responsible for his own family.

A

Son

· *Needs a* ·

DAD

WHO KNOWS HOW TO HAVE FUN.

·

*who will show him
that love is unselfish.*

·

WHO IS WILLING TO MAKE
SACRIFICES FOR HIS FAMILY.

A
Son
· Needs a ·
DAD

TO WRESTLE WITH HIM IN THE GRASS.

....

to take him fishing.

....

TO HELP HIM BUILD A TREE HOUSE.

A

Son

· Needs a ·

DAD

TO TELL HIM OFTEN THAT HE IS LOVED.

·

*to teach him when to lead
and when to follow.*

·

TO SHOW HIM UNCONDITIONAL LOVE.

A

Son

· *Needs a* ·

DAD

....

who will help his mother.

....

A

Son

· *Needs a* ·

DAD

....

to let him be his equal now and then.

....

TO SHOW HIM HOW TO TIE A NECKTIE.

A

Son

· Needs a ·

DAD

to build a loving house on a foundation
of wisdom and understanding.

·

TO HELP EASE THE BURDENS
THAT WEIGH HEAVILY ON HIM.

·

to teach him not to let pride
get in the way of listening.

A

Son

· *Needs a* ·

DAD

· ·

to teach him to be accountable
for his wrongdoings.

· ·

A

Son

· Needs a ·

DAD

to teach him that strength is
best expressed with restraint.

·

TO LEAD HIM TOWARD FAITH.

A

Son

· *Needs a* ·

DAD

....

to teach him how things work.

....

TO TEACH HIM TO GIVE MORE THAN HE TAKES.

A

Son

· Needs a ·

DAD

who will give the comfort of
protection and affection.

·

TO TEACH HIM THAT HE DOES NOT
ALWAYS NEED TO BE IN CONTROL.

A

Son

• Needs a •

DAD

....

to tell him it is okay to admit his mistakes.

....

A

Son

· *Needs a* ·

DAD

to teach him to think about
consequences before he acts.

.

TO TEACH HIM TO ACCEPT
THE DIFFERENCES IN OTHERS.

A

Son

· *Needs a* ·

DAD

TO TEACH HIM TO APOLOGIZE
FOR RECKLESS WORDS.

·

*to pull him back when he is
headed in the wrong direction.*

A

Son

· *Needs a* ·

DAD

*to go with him on
imaginary adventures.*

···

TO HELP HIM FIND HIS WAY.

···

A
Son
· Needs a ·
DAD

TO ENCOURAGE HIM WHEN HE
MEETS WITH DISAPPOINTMENT.

·

*to tell him that it is wise
to seek advice.*

·

TO TELL HIM THAT IGNORANCE
IS NOT AN EXCUSE.

A

Son

· *Needs a* ·

DAD

··

who can be playful and silly.

··

A

Son

· Needs a ·

DAD

TO HELP HIM UNDERSTAND IT ISN'T
NECESSARY TO BE LIKE EVERYONE ELSE.

to teach him to stand up for himself.

A

Son

· *Needs a* ·

DAD

....

to make the family whole.

....

A

Son

· Needs a ·

DAD

WHO WILL NOT EXPECT THE
UNREASONABLE FROM HIM.

·

to urge him to pursue worthy goals.

·

TO TEACH HIM TO TAKE PRIDE IN
PROVIDING FOR THE FAMILY.

A

Son

· Needs a ·

DAD

....

who will be there for him when he needs help.

....

A
Son
· *Needs a* ·
DAD

TO TAKE HIM CAMPING.

·

*to encourage patriotism
and civic responsibility.*

·

TO TEACH HIM HOW TO
FIX THINGS HIMSELF.

A

Son

· *Needs a* ·

DAD

· ·

to take him to baseball games.

· ·

SO THAT HE WILL HAVE AT LEAST
ONE HERO HE CAN DEPEND ON.

A
Son
· Needs a ·
DAD

· ·

to teach him that respect
must be earned.

· ·

A

Son

Needs a

DAD

TO TEACH HIM TO HONOR
THE WOMAN WHO LOVES HIM.

·

to teach him to be honest at all times.

·

TO TEACH HIM THAT FORGIVING IS
ALWAYS THE RIGHT THING TO DO.

A

Son

· *Needs a* ·

DAD

··

who welcomes self-expression.

··

TO NURTURE HIS INDEPENDENCE.

A
Son
· Needs a ·
DAD

who will show him affection
without hesitation.

A

Son

· *Needs a* ·

DAD

TO TEACH HIM TO BE
RESPECTFUL OF WOMEN.

•

to teach him how to be a gentleman.

•

TO HELP HIM PLAN FOR HIS FUTURE.

A

Son

· *Needs a* ·

DAD

....

to tell him that he is proud of him.

....

A

Son

· Needs a ·

DAD

TO TELL HIM THAT THERE IS
NO DISGRACE IN LOSING.

·

*to help him try again after
he has stumbled.*

·

TO SHOW HIM PATIENCE.

A

Son

· Needs a ·

DAD

....

to teach him to always
give a good day's work.

....

A

Son

· Needs a ·

DAD

TO TALK WITH ABOUT THE TOUGH
DECISIONS HE WILL FACE.

·

*to show him how to
control his temper.*

·

TO HELP HIM LEARN

FROM HIS MISTAKES.

A

Son

· Needs a ·

DAD

....

to be a doting grandfather to his children.

....

A
Son
· *Needs a* ·
DAD

··

who will help him discover
his place in life.

··

A

Son

· *Needs a* ·

DAD

to comfort him when he cries.

．

TO SHOW HIM THE MEANING
OF THE WORD *RELIABLE*.

A
Son
· Needs a ·
DAD

who will protect him when he is not
strong enough to protect himself.

A

Son

· Needs a ·

DAD

*to share with him the wisdom
he has not yet acquired.*

.

TO GIVE HIM THE GENTLE PUSHES
THAT HELP HIM GROW.

A

Son

· *Needs a* ·

DAD

....

to encourage him when he is in doubt of himself.

....

A

Son

· Needs a ·

DAD

TO SHOW HIM THE DIFFERENCE BETWEEN
BEING FIRM AND BEING STUBBORN.

·

to teach him not to use others
for his own benefit.

·

TO PROVIDE MORAL GUIDANCE AS
HE BECOMES A MAN.

A

Son

· Needs a ·

DAD

....

who allows him to question.

....

A

Son

· Needs a ·

DAD

TO SHOW HIM HOW TO COMPROMISE.

to stand with him the day he marries.

TO SHOW HIM HOW TO BE
A GOOD HUSBAND.

A
Son
· Needs a ·
DAD

....

to teach him that family is
more important than work.

....

A

Son

· *Needs a* ·

DAD

WHO WILL DISCIPLINE HIM FIRMLY AND
FAIRLY, WHILE LOVING HIM RELENTLESSLY.

·

*who will teach him to avoid
selfish temptations.*

A
Son
· *Needs a* ·
DAD

....

to help him face his challenges
with confidence.

....

A
Son
Needs a
DAD

TO SHOW HIM HOW TO LOVE OTHERS,
EVEN WHEN IT IS HARD.

*to teach him how to maintain
dignity in difficult times.*

A

Son

· *Needs a* ·

DAD

....

to provide the guidance that will
steer him from trouble.

....

A

Son

· Needs a ·

DAD

TO TEACH HIM TO RECOGNIZE
THE TRUTH AND REWARD IT.

·

*to teach him to recognize sincerity
and encourage it.*

·

TO BE THE STANDARD BY WHICH HE WILL
LATER MEASURE HIMSELF.

A

Son

· Needs a ·

DAD

to be the role model for the
father he will become.

A

Son

• *Needs a* •

DAD

because without him he will have
less in his life than he deserves.

· ACKNOWLEDGMENTS ·

This book could not have been written without the support and generosity of many people. I offer a special thanks to the sons and dads who shared their stories with me, who became my friends during this process, and who helped me find the heart of the matter, the profound and nearly endless reasons why sons need their dads. I was deeply touched by the love I witnessed in the time I spent with you.

I wish to thank Ron Pitkin and the staff at Cumberland House, including my editor, Lisa Taylor, who once again pushed me to make sure this book became what it could be. I also want to give special thanks to Julie Jayne, whose faith in each book has been a key contributor to the success of the series. Julie, you have my deepest appreciation and warmest regards.

· TO CONTACT THE AUTHOR ·

Write in care of the publisher:
Gregory E. Lang c/o Sourcebooks, Inc.
P.O. Box 4410
Naperville, IL 60567-4410

Email the author or visit his website:
gregoryelang@gmail.com
www.gregoryelang.com